USE AND ABUSE OF HISTORY

USE AND ABUSE

OF HISTORY

by Pieter Geyl

ARCHON BOOKS, 1970

ISBN: 0 208 00827 6
Library of Congress Catalog Card Number: 77-113016
Printed in the United States of America

PREFATORY NOTE

$\mathcal{I}$ CANNOT let this little book go out into the world without expressing my gratitude to Yale University for inviting me to deliver the Terry Lectures for 1954. I am grateful not only for the honor thus conferred upon me, but for the encouragement the invitation meant to me to present in a connected form ideas upon which my mind had been running since the war but to which I had so far only given somewhat scattered expression, always in immediate connection with concrete historical or historiographical problems—witness my *Napoleon For and Against* and a number of essays and lectures now collected under the title *Debates with Historians*.

I shall always preserve a happy memory of my brief stay at New Haven in October 1954 and of the cordial and stimulating reception accorded me by colleagues and students.

A word of particular thanks is due to David Horne, who helped me in preparing the lectures for print and, while showing great forbearance when I proved intractable, made a number of suggestions which I gladly accepted.

P. G.

Utrecht
April 7, 1955

CHAPTER ONE

ℐN WHAT FOLLOWS I write not as a philosopher but as a historian. If I venture to deal with some general aspects of history, I shall not feel compelled to analyze all my assumptions. No doubt a fundamental view of life in its relation to eternity directs my thinking, but I shall allow it to be deduced or guessed at from my treatment of the subject. As a matter of method I shall be practical and concrete, as befits my calling. I shall argue from my own experience and look at the problems as they have presented themselves to me in the course of a lengthening life spent, if I may say so, not merely in studying the past but in watching the world around me and occasionally, in a modest way, trying to take part in its struggles.

This does not mean that I am setting out to present a chapter of autobiography. I shall try to integrate my personal observations and pragmatic solutions with the general trends of historical thinking and practice. Since I am fairly representative of the modern student of history—at least so I believe—it should prove a perfectly natural undertaking. Moreover, being what I am and writing on history, I shall feel the need of historical background: it is our ingrained belief that as problems present themselves today they can be probed only if we place them in perspective; it is one of the uses of history about which I shall have more to say.

History tries to fulfill certain of our permanent and profound needs as civilized and social beings. From the very beginning, as soon as groups of human beings freed themselves from the shackles of primitivity or began to dispute—however partially and tentatively—the despotism of custom, they took to noting down striking events and the names of leading members. These earliest monuments of history served more purposes than one. They were intended to glorify kings or priests or warriors and by their glory to shed luster on the dynasty, the church, or the state. But at the same time the bare facts which they helped to fix constituted a knowledge useful for the stability of society and its institutions.

There has been this antinomy from the beginning of history: change, movement were the indispensable conditions for its birth, yet one of the main purposes to which it was immediately put was the prevention of change and movement. Substitute "regulation" for "prevention" and you have the purpose of what was to develop eventually into a wealth of literature. In early times the epic, tempestuously bursting the bounds of reality, even of probability, is nevertheless a kind of history, and the one in which feelings of loyalty or communal pride take the lead. The chronicle is the form in which the idea of the usefulness of factual notation predominates. Both appeal to feelings, which they at the same time rouse to consciousness, not only of veneration or of awe, but of disinterested delight in the spectacle of things past, a feeling of wonder, an aesthetic feeling.

There is another craving which the human mind since early times has attempted to satisfy by turning to history. Events are interpreted, or they are related into a significant whole, so as to throw light on the great mystery of man's fate on earth and the way it is influenced or directed by the divine powers. In both epic and chronicle this element is frequently found, and the holy books of many religions are replete with history. It is not always possible to draw a clear distinction between these various types of writings. The historical books of the Old Testament partake of the epic as well as the chronicle, while at the same time intended to reveal God's disposal of human affairs. But we have a motive here which has been fertile enough to bring forth a whole literature of its own.

The earliest example in the Christian era is the Revelation of St. John. In the right hand of Him who sits upon the throne of Heaven the author sees the book sealed with seven seals, which no man can unseal, containing the history of mankind. When revealed by the Lamb, this proves to consist of a succession of disasters, the punishment for idolatry and sin; but the predestined end is the bliss of the elect.

A few centuries later Augustine wrote the first true philosophy of history. The thesis of *De civitate Dei* was clearly inspired by the spirit of the Book of Revelation, only it was worked out with a much closer attention to the actual phenomena of man's communal life on earth.[1] It was this great work that impressed successive generations of readers with the conception of the unity and the spiritual significance of human history. Augustine represents history as the struggle between the City of God and the City of Satan, the outcome of which is never in doubt and judged by which the activities of rulers and states, their manifestations of power, and the vicissitudes of temporal victory or defeat sink into nothingness.

I must not and I shall not in this essay attempt to give a brief history of historiography. The purposes

1. Augustinus, 354–430; bishop of Hippo in North Africa. *De civitate Dei*, written under the effect of Alaric's sack of Rome in 410, was completed in 426.

for which men study history and which in the early days of civilization were separately linked with the chronicle, the epic, and the books of religion still hold the field. They can appear in an infinite variety of shapes; they can be served in an infinite variety of ways. It would be a fascinating study to follow the development step by step, all the time trying to keep in mind these fundamental divisions which, I repeat, far from excluding one another often have their dividing lines blurred or are inextricably combined. The prevalence of one particular tendency in a given period and of another at some other time, and their connections with the general trends of thought, would make a tempting subject. Instead, I shall confine myself to a few rapid indications mainly relating to modern times.

The Renaissance ushered in a period in which historical studies took wing. Documents were unearthed and published; local, national, party, or sectarian histories, memoirs, and biographies were written in large numbers. Often these were based on serious research and the material and its interpretation were increasingly subjected to criticism. The interesting question for our present purpose is, first of all, what was the driving force behind this great intellectual effort? What was it that men hoped to find in history?

The Renaissance brought about a strong upwelling of the critical attitude of mind and caused attention to be concentrated on human factors for the explanation of human affairs. The Reformation, on the other hand, led to a reassertion of the theological view. All over Europe writers in both camps used history to show the working of God's providence, each, of course, in accordance with his own particular prejudices and predilections. *God's Way with the Netherlands* is the title of a book in which as late as 1752 a clergyman of the Dutch Reformed Church worked out a theological version of Dutch history.[2] The title could serve for the text of innumerable sermons, the tenor of which would be the prosperity and the power of the little Republic as evidence of God's having chosen the Dutch people, as in olden times he chose the Israelites, to be the shining example among nations, while adversity and disasters would be explained as tokens of His wrath for backsliding or for lukewarm faith.

The most famous work in which in this period

2. Arnoldus Rotterdam, *Gods weg met Nederland*, 1752. The Princes of Orange were often pictured as being very specially the chosen agents of God's will in history. So A. R. saw God's special intervention in the elevation, in 1747, of William IV to the offices of his forefathers, after these had been in abeyance ever since the death of William III in 1702, while the untimely death of the Prince only a few years later, in 1751, seemed to him directly due to "our atheism and ungodliness, our hypocrisy and lifeless religion, our profanation of God's name and day, our pride and self-sufficiency," etc. "With all these shortcomings we have exhausted the divine patience."

the whole of history is surveyed from the supernatural point of view is Bossuet's *Discours sur l'histoire universelle*,[3] which owes a great deal to Augustine's *De civitate Dei*. But although there is a vast literature reflecting these ideas, it is a special literature, of edification rather than instruction. The general run of works of history, while occasionally, in an aside as it were, making their bow to the theological interpretation, on the whole continue to proceed on the assumption that human affairs are shaped by human factors. As time went on, the secular attitude became more self-assertive and even aggressive, but even then, and indeed down to the present day, one will frequently find the two interpretations, which might seem mutually exclusive, amicably existing side by side in the same mind.

After the changes caused by the Reformation in state and church, the period became one of comparative stability. The public mind was for a long time preponderantly conservative. "It is the duty of a good citizen to preserve the state in its present condition and not to wish for change." [4] Innumerable

3. 1681. Jacques Bénigne Bossuet, 1627–1704, bishop of Meaux, one of the great masters of French prose and an influential eccelsiastical statesman.

4. "Boni civis est presentem statum reipublicae tueri eumque mutatum nolle." For seventeenth-century instances see *Stadhouderschap*, n. 6, below; for an eighteenth-century instance— the well-known historian Jan Wagenaar using the phrase in 1757—see my treatise *De Wittenoorlog*, Mededelingen van de Kon. Ned. Akademie van Wetenschappen, 1953.

times have I found the Latin tag giving expression to this sentiment quoted in Dutch political literature of the seventeenth and eighteenth centuries; significantly, it occurs in that of both the parties whose struggles constituted so large a part of Dutch history during the period. Grotius, in a youthful work, expressed the same idea in a striking manner, unconsciously revealing the quality of his mind (for in the metaphor he used, a later view of profound importance is anticipated). To change laws, he said, is a risky undertaking (and for "laws" we may read "constitution"): "It is better to acquiesce in existing laws even if they are not the best imaginable. Laws, like plants, need time to strike roots, and when you transplant them too frequently, their strength and vitality become sapped." [5]

History to those generations seemed useful first of all because by means of it everybody could know

5. Grotius (Hugo de Groot, 1583–1645) played a part in the politics of the Dutch Republic as pensionary of Rotterdam and adviser of the Advocate of Holland, Oldenbarnevelt; imprisoned after the crisis of 1618, he made his escape in 1621 and spent the rest of his life in exile. He enjoyed a European fame as a writer on theology and law, especially international law: *De jure belli ac pacis*, 1625; *De antiquitate Batavorum*, 1610; the Dutch translation of the latter, in which he took a hand, bore the title: *Van de oudheydt der Batavische, nu Hollandsche Republique*. I speak in the text of "the Estates assembly of Holland." The term "States of Holland" is more usual but lends itself to misunderstanding. States, *états* (in German: *Stände*) means of course estates, that is, classes.

his rights. The state itself felt the need of the antiquity which was the great title to respect. In the work of Grotius quoted above, written in 1610, hardly a generation since the revolt from which had sprung the Dutch Republic, the young man undertook to show how venerably old, in spite of appearances, was the existing condition of things in his own province of Holland (one of the seven sovereign entities making up the Dutch Republic). The sovereignty of the Estates assembly of Holland—so he gravely sets out—dated from medieval times, long before the revolt; more, the Estates simply continued to exercise the sovereign powers held by the popular assembly of the ancient Batavians at the beginning of the Christian era; the Stadtholder, the princely official of Grotius' own day, dignified and influential yet devoid of any powers that might detract from the sovereignty of the Estates, was in all essentials the successor of the medieval counts and chosen kings of the Batavians. Speaking from the point of view of modern scholarship, the argument is ludicrous; but ignorance of the true facts of medieval and premedieval history was universal among Grotius' contemporaries, and his little treatise, *Antiquity of the Batavian Republic* (that is, of the province of Holland), was eagerly welcomed for the support it gave to the existing state of affairs. History was a great conserving power—but it appears from this instance that history in order to ful-

fill that function had at times to make very free with
the past.

And of course history, which could be made to
prove such unlikely things, was never able, even
when everybody swore by its authority, to make an
end of discussion. Even in that period of relative
stability all movement could not be arrested. Even
in that period of acquiescence people's minds could
not be prevented from conceiving grievances and
desires for change. No doubt the discontented and
the restless shared the universal respect for the past
and its superior wisdom, but it was easy for them,
too, to find in history what they needed. They had
only to search the variegated records to turn up
something that seemed to justify their contentions
and ambitions.

Everybody could learn from history to know his
rights?

Prove, for instance, that a preceding line of kings,
the Tudors, had been able to do certain things without the concurrence, or even against the wishes, of
Parliament and you proved that in the struggle between Charles I and the House of Commons right
was on the king's side. The trouble was that in England Parliament had on other occasions stood up for
its rights. Had it not, indeed, made and unmade
kings?

History, then, was not only a conserving power;
it served as a weapon in party strife. In countries

where public life was dominated by party division —in England, in the Dutch Republic, indeed for purposes of controversy between Catholicism and Protestantism all over Europe—history was ransacked for material that might support the case of one side or discredit the past doings or long defunct leading personalities of the other. Not an unknown phenomenon in later ages, it may be thought; yet the way in which it was done and the proportions which historic allusions or expositions assumed in the political rough-and-tumble of seventeenth-century party warfare does seem surprising to the modern observer and is well fitted to make him realize the relationship toward the past which was characteristic of those generations.

It is perhaps most easily defined by pointing out its difference from our own outlook. What they lacked was awareness of distance, of a general "otherness" of earlier ages as regards not only circumstances but mentality. The concept of growth and development, in which change is implied and with which we are so familiar, was to them almost unknown. Even if, as we saw, it flashed upon an unusual mind like that of Grotius (and I might quote others), no one made it the basis of an all-embracing interpretation of history. This mental attitude enabled them without scruple to apply old instances to their own times.

Some years ago I studied a famous controversy

about the constitution of the province of Holland in the 1660's.[6] The attention given to the misdeeds of former Stadtholders (or, in the pamphlets of the other side, of the great Grandpensionary of an earlier generation, Barneveld) struck me as so excessive that the entire argument seemed to bear a look of unreality. The actual political problems were hardly dealt with directly; they were approached by conventional roundabout ways. And not only the precedents of the republican period were adduced, which were after all comparable, but even the alleged misdeeds of medieval counts were used to belabor later Stadtholders, as if the radically different position of the latter were foreshadowed by the former. But we have only to remember Grotius' *De antiquitate*.

Here we have another trait typical of historical feeling such as the seventeenth century knew it. They looked to the past for prefigurations, for symbols, of contemporary events or personalities. Not only—not even in the first place—to decry, but to do homage. History was to them a treasure house from which could be taken beautiful and dignified images fit, by way of similitude, to elevate and decorate the present. The painters reveled in this kind

6. My study resulted in a treatise which appeared in Mededelingen der Kon. Ned. Akademie van Wetenschappen (1947), under the title: *Het stadhouderschap in de partij-literatuur onder De Witt*.

of historical symbolism. And it was not national history which furnished the most shining examples, but the history of Israel and the history of Rome. I mentioned that the Dutch Calvinists, in speaking of the country where their faith had come to be dominant as the "chosen country," loved to apply to it the most striking phraseology of the Old Testament. The general tendency toward thinking in parallels helps to explain how this went down so easily. Frenchmen could not do justice to the Great King's glory without dragging in Caesar or Alexander. It needs little imagination to realize that opposing interests could each find what suited them in the Old Testament and Roman history as readily as in the various periods of national history. The Estates party in Holland appealed to the Judges in Israel, while the Orangists loved to recall the Kings—instituted by God in his wrath, as they were reminded by the republicans. And when faced with the historic claims of landlords and nobility, the English social revolutionaries of the fifteenth century went as far back as Adam and Eve, with one stroke thrusting aside all history:

> When Adam delved, and Eve span,
> Who was then the gentleman?

Not, however, in this symbolic fashion or for these ceremonial or conserving or party purposes only was history used. It was regarded as a great textbook of morals and statecraft. "Histories make men wise," said Bacon,[7] and historians without number presented their books as a contribution toward the education of princes or statesmen or indeed anyone anxious to learn how the world wags. You may think, why not? I agree; I, too, set store by the educative value of history, and I shall later on have more to say about it. Only, the seventeenth-century historian was apt to draw his moral and point his lesson in a way that to the modern reader seems to make light of the profound difference between the ages as well as of the infinite complexity of circumstances in which every decision is taken and every deed done. Nevertheless, that the attention given to the past in so many forms did broaden the outlook and enrich civilization cannot for a moment be doubted. And although violent partisanship or all too naive pragmatism were responsible for a good many deficiencies in the works produced, even so the interest they aroused acted as a fillip to historical scholarship, inspiring serious investigation, whetting the faculty of criticism.

In fact, no characterization of the mentality of a period is complete which does not leave room for exceptions, and the exceptions are often important in that they announce later developments. People

7. Francis Bacon, 1561–1626; statesman and philosopher. His dictum on history is in "On Studies," *Essays;* quoted by G. J. Renier, *History, Its Purpose and Method* (1950), p. 19.

n the seventeenth century seemed little aware of the completely different social habits and mentality of 'ormer ages. When the great Dutch poet Vondel wrote a play on the rebellion of the Batavians against their Roman conquerors, he could make of the leaders nothing but the ratiocinating citizens, conscious of their rights, whom he knew around him in mid-seventeenth-century Amsterdam.[8] But Rembrandt's great painting of the Conjuration represents the one-eyed chief and his comrades as the terrible barbaric conspirators they probably were; at any rate his imagination loved to bring to life something utterly different from the peaceable, law-stricken society in which he lived—with the result that the Amsterdam burgomasters for whose new town hall the picture was intended were aghast at seeing these honorable ancestors, prototypes of the fighters for freedom in the war against Spain, treated so disrespectfully, and Rembrandt's greatest "history painting" has had to find a resting place in Stockholm.[9]

Shakespeare can also be cited. Countless times it has been affirmed that in his history plays he presented Elizabethans masquerading as Romans or medieval barons. To me the fascinating thing is to

8. Joost van den Vondel, *b.* 1587. The play mentioned in the text, *De Batavische Gebroeders*, is one of his weakest; he was a prolific writer, in middle and old age dominating his period.

9. On Rembrandt's painting of the Conspiracy of Julius (or Claudius) Civilis, see Seymour Slive, *Rembrandt and his Critics* (1953), p. 77 f. Rembrandt, 1606–69.

observe, on the contrary, his unusual sensitivity to historical atmosphere. He may have dressed up his characters in the wrong costumes (as indeed Rembrandt did also), but how different is the general tone of feeling and character in, say, *Antony and Cleopatra*—foreign, southern—from those of *Henry IV*—English to the core. And compare *Macbeth* with *The Merchant of Venice;* who will not see that Shakespeare tried to bring out remoteness in time and barbaric society in the one case against an overripe, sophisticated civilization in the other? This capacity, indeed this desire, to evolve backgrounds in time and space is what distinguishes Shakespeare from most of the dramatists of his own and the succeeding generation, from Corneille and Racine for example.[10]

In other respects, too, one must not speak too dogmatically about seventeenth-century characteristics. The general tendency was to accept the Old Testament reverently as the inspired history of God's own people; yet Spinoza advocated a fearless historical and philological examination.[11] The general tendency was to idealize Roman history; yet (if I may take another Dutchman to illustrate my

10. I wrote more fully on Shakespeare as a historian in "Shakespeare als geschiedschrijver," an essay published in *Nieuw Vlaams Tijdschrift* (Antwerp, 1947–48), reprinted in my volume of essays *Tochten en Toernooien* (1950), pp. 1–92. Shakespeare, 1564–1616; Corneille, 1606–84; Racine, 1639–99.

11. Spinoza, of Amsterdam, 1632–77.

point) that most interesting writer on economics and politics, De la Court, in 1662 protested against the advice to "follow the old Romans' example" and in general to regard all that was old as venerable: "antiquity," he says, "does not warrant wisdom; let us follow the example set by *wise* Romans." And as a general warning against monarchy he drew a terrible picture of crimes and horrors committed by many Roman emperors.[12]

Toward the close of the seventeenth century history traversed a crisis. Doubts were expressed on many sides concerning the value of a discipline so incapable of achieving certainty. Did not history prove herself the obedient servant of every ruler, of either of the two sides of every conflict? Did she not supply facts to suit every party so long as it could ask for them with a show of power? Did not the facts of history turn out to be the merest foppery? French authors especially indulged in this mood of skepticism, but elsewhere, too, the mocking or despairing tones of Pyrrhonism were heard, and when one looks at the results achieved, the doubts seem justified. Yet the great labor of research went on undismayed; in the next century the pace was

12. Pieter de la Court, Leyden textile manufacturer, 1618–85. His most important work is *Interest van Holland* (1662), of which a French translation was published under the very misleading title *Mémoires de Jean de Witt*. The remark cited in the text is from a pamphlet of his and was quoted before in *Stadhouderschap*, p. 21.

even accelerated; and it was this more than the philosophic or argumentative attempts to disprove the case of the skeptics that helped to maintain and strengthen the position of history. Not only did the accumulation of authentic materials grow, but, more than that, the gradual elaboration of methods and standards of criticism inspired confidence.

In the meantime the spirit in which the more reflective minds began to handle the knowledge thus acquired and made ready for use underwent a change: the critical attitude of mind extended to the whole meaning and purpose of history. The purely secular interpretation came to prevail more and more, although the theological interpretation was never completely driven off the field. It continued to flourish in its own preserves—in encyclicals and sermons, in tracts and orations—and also, as we shall see, it lent itself, paradoxically enough, to secularization and was adapted out of all recognition. But the striking thing in this period was that there was no longer this submissiveness in the attitude toward the past, as if it alone had a command of true wisdom, and as if history, therefore, were entitled to lay down the law. The other view—of the past as an instructive spectacle—now confidently took charge of the field. The philosophy of enlightenment was in open revolt against the despotism of history. Instead of being the slave of history, it wanted freely and for its own purposes to use her. Reason and the eternal laws of nature were in the future to be the guiding lights of mankind.

Rousseau blamed Grotius for constantly establishing the right by the fact: "No method," he observes, "could be more favorable to tyrants." [13] Diderot said: "Some may think that a knowledge of history should precede that of morality. I am not of that opinion: it seems to me more useful and expedient to possess the idea of the just and the unjust before possessing a knowledge of the actions and the men to whom one ought to apply it." [14] And so we find Voltaire using history with complete freedom of mind, without any consciousness of being in any way bound by it. The *Essai sur les moeurs* is an important work in the history of civilization.[15] Voltaire widened the boundaries of history by giving attention to religion and social habits, and of the most diverse nations and ages, going far outside Europe. But he did it without disinterested enjoyment of what is different, without in any way emotionally associating himself with the colorful, genuine mani-

13. J. J. Rousseau, 1712–78. It is especially in the *Contrat social* (1762), from which the quotation is taken, that Rousseau tries to build up "les principes du droit publique" by means of natural law and without reference to history.

14. Denis Diderot, 1713–84. Quoted by Carl Becker, *The Heavenly City of the Eighteenth Century Philosophers*, 1932.

15. F. M. Arouet, 1694–1778, as a young man assumed the name Voltaire. The *Essai sur les moeurs*, a large work, appeared in 1756.

19

festations of life in shapes foreign to his own time and country. He is, throughout, the eighteenth-century Frenchman, comparing, mocking, if not at those comic backward medieval people or barbarians then at the stupid arrangements or prejudices of his contemporaries, to whom he holds up, for instance, enlightened and tolerant China. He does show an acute awareness of contrasts, but always allied to it there is the intention, the tendency, toward reform. "Of all the events of that period," he writes in a chapter on France during the tenth and eleventh centuries, "the one most worthy of the citizen's attention is the excommunication of King Dagobert." It goes without saying that the incident affords him an excuse for digressions on papal abuse of power and the like. That which is "worthy of the citizen's attention": the criterion is significant. That which, in other words, throws light on the politics of today or can be of assistance in the party struggle.

This, I repeat, was far from being an entirely novel attitude of mind. The Enlightenment had its roots deep in the past, indeed in human nature. The quotation from De la Court, in which he made a distinction between *old* and *wise* and exhorted us to be guided by the example not of the former but of the latter, implied an outlook not fundamentally different from that of Voltaire. Reason is an essential attribute of man, and it has always been apt to lead the enterprising or the zealous into conflict with history. The course of absolutist, centralizing, and equalizing monarchy, from the later Middle Ages on, was strewn with disputes between, on the one hand, royal reformers appealing to equity and the good of society or the state, and on the other, privileged classes clinging to their rights hallowed by precedent or prescription. But now the idea that a new day had broken took hold of an entire generation of intellectuals: their predecessors seemed to them to have been living in the darkness of superstition, and the worst of their illusions had been this worship of injustices and absurdities just because they were rooted in history. It was the idea of natural rights, "truths held to be self-evident" (to use the confident phrase of the Declaration of Independence), that inspired the Americans to set up a new government and make a constitution in defiance of history. A century earlier the Glorious Revolution in England had limited its aim to the removal of the tyrant; it had been careful of historic rights and precedents and indeed professed to be anxious to restore and preserve rather than to subvert. The other mood, observable in the American Revolution, very shortly afterward triumphed much more absolutely in France. "Let us destroy everything," exclaimed a deputy in the National Assembly; "yes, everything, for everything has to be remade." [16] And another deputy cries, "The day of the Revelation has ar-

16. Quoted by Burke in his *Reflections;* see below, n. 19.

rived, the bones of the victims found in the Bastille have risen at the call of French liberty. They testify against centuries of oppression and of death, prophesying the regeneration of human nature and of the life of the nations." [17]

The French Revolution, which felt the need of a new Year One and a new calendar, was a revolution against history. Without attempting at this stage to speculate upon the respective rights of history and of revolution, I cannot refrain from remarking that the abuse of history in the preceding generations, the clinging to outworn privilege and law and pretending that they must be sacred because they are old, undeniably constituted a very real provocation. But we can see no less clearly now that when the movement, carried along on its own passion and impetus, attacked not the abuse only but history itself, it ran into disaster. The attempt to set up all at once a philosophers' heaven on earth led to the awful tyranny of a minority dictatorship first, of a military despotism next. For meanwhile the claim to bring the new gospel of salvation to all nations had landed France in a war with the whole of Europe, of which catastrophe was the only possible ending.

History had her revenge in more subtle ways than that. First of all, the revolutionaries themselves, talking as if their doings were an unheard-of novelty

17. Quoted by Jules Michelet, *Histoire de la Révolution française,* 1847–53.

opening a new and in fact the decisive and final chapter in the world's annals, had insensibly fallen into the old ways traced for them by the kings and their governments in the benighted centuries past. Tocqueville, long after the Revolution, was the first to point out in detail that their internal reforms of centralized and simplified administration followed the lines of monarchical tradition.[18] A generation later Albert Sorel showed how their foreign policy, too, in spite of all the generous phrases about liberating the peoples and instructing the world in the new wisdom revealed to the French, soon came to lean on the old traditions of expansionism and *reason of state*—traditions left behind by generations of royal diplomats.

Tocqueville wrote in the 1850's; Sorel's first volume appeared in 1887. But as early as 1790 the first great pronouncement against the Revolution, Burke's famous *Reflections*, had in effect been an appeal to history.[19] The work strikingly illustrates the strength of that method as well as the dangers inherent in it. Disgusted as he is by the spectacle of the violence of the mob, the presumptuous enthusiasm of the theoricians, and the indignities suffered

18. Alexis de Tocqueville, 1805–59; French statesman and historian. *La Démocratie en Amérique*, 1835–40; *L'ancien régime et la Révolution*, 1856–57. Cf. below, Ch. 2, w. 2.

19. Edmund Burke, 1729–97; British statesman and philosopher. There is an ed. of *Reflections on the Revolution in France* (1790) in the Everyman Library.

by king, nobility, and clergy, Burke is tempted to minimize grievances and ridicule projected reforms which were, in spite of all failures, permanently and in many ways beneficially to alter the face of France and Europe. For the immediate future, nevertheless, his predictions of chaos, tyranny, and military despotism proved wonderfully clear-sighted.

In any case the contrast between the rationalistic or theoretical (as he put it, "metaphysical") and the practical, circumstantial, historical view of state and society and politics was most impressively stated. To represent the Revolution in France as a better edition of the English Revolution of 1688 (as Dr. Price and his fellow sympathizers with the French had done) was in his view an outrage.

> The [Glorious] Revolution was made to preserve our *ancient* indisputable laws and liberties, and that *ancient* constitution of government which is our only security for law and liberty. . . . The very idea of the fabrication of a new government is enough to fill us with disgust and horror. We wished at the period of the Revolution, and do now wish, to derive all we possess as *an inheritance from our forefathers.*

The collective wisdom of the generations; the wise looking for the latent wisdom in general prejudices rather than rashly ridiculing them; reason supported by tradition and better able to maintain liberty when strengthened by the consciousness of unity with our predecessors—these are some of the concepts Burke opposes to the "nakedness and solitude of metaphysical abstraction." Without those aids "men would become little better than the flies of a summer," and he sorrows about the folly of the French, who take a perverse pleasure in regarding themselves "as a people of yesterday, as a nation of low-born servile wretches until the emancipating year 1789."

The conservatism of the seventeenth century is here transformed into a system of thought of infinitely richer possibilities. It has been infused with an awareness of the indispensable value of nonrational forces in the life of a community. In Burke's mystical union embracing the generations, the idea of growth, still rudimentary with Grotius, appears at last ready to blossom out.

The times were propitious. The whole of Herder's work had been animated by that idea.[20] In these same years of the French Revolution he rounded off his system in his *Ideën zur Philosophie der Geschichte*. The affinity with Burke is unmis-

20. J. G. Herder, 1744–1803. Wrote extensively on literature, directing attention especially to folk songs and looking for the national spirit in literary works. His friendship with Goethe had importance from the point of view of intellectual or cultural history. His *Ideën zur Geschichte der Menschheit* appeared 1784–91.

takable, and yet there is a difference. Herder had had to adapt his new view of history to the inchoate conditions of Germany. To him the moving force of history could not be that which governed the thinking of Burke: a politically fully developed nation, with its precise recollections and traditions of constitutional precedents; to Herder it was the nation, spread over a number of states, with inborn qualities and inspirations, a given entity, transcending human reason or will power. Rousseau himself, with that curious ambivalence which is characteristic of him, had stimulated not only rationalism but sentiment. At the very moment of the Revolution, which proclaimed itself to be the triumph of reason, Romanticism was in the air. But soon it was more particularly the derailment of the Revolution, the disillusionment of its supporters, the satisfaction of its opponents, which gave rise to a deliberate and systematic reappraisal of history.

Had not the free play of reason been proved powerless to direct the course of human affairs? The question arose in many minds long before the downfall of Napoleon, but with particular insistence when *it* led to a restoration of much that had been abolished in the name of the new philosophy. While propagating its ideas and spreading abroad its new forms of administration and law, the Revolution as embodied by Napoleon, had roused against itself deep-rooted instincts, loyalties of various kinds religion, nationalism. Must it not be accepted as the task of history to trace these forces, and was it any use, was it not going against the immutable order of human affairs, to call them before the court of fallible Reason and to want them other than they were? It is true that much was saved from the bankruptcy of the Revolution, and in some of its aspects the Restoration might rather be termed a consolidation of the new order. It was still to be a period of strife, therefore, strife between revolution and counter-revolution.

This continuing conflict added bitterness to the mood in which the problem was tackled by counter-revolutionary writers in all European countries. But the implications for history transcended the political issue, and it was especially in Germany that these were investigated, both in theory and in practice. It was German historical thinking in the first decades of the nineteenth century that transformed the historical outlook of the whole of the Western world; and in spite of all the heated discussions and the changes and refinements and heresies that have since occurred, it may be said, transformed permanently.

CHAPTER TWO

*E*IGHTEENTH-CENTURY Rationalism, impatient with conditions as they actually were, ready to subject every tradition and every generally held opinion to fearless criticism, intent on improvement and reform, found itself already, as I have said above, opposed by counterforces which soon gained immensely in strength and confidence from the discomfiture of the Revolution and Napoleonic Empire.

There was widespread response to the sarcasm directed by a writer like Count De Maistre at the idea of man being able with his feeble reason to re-form the political circumstances in which his lot was cast.[1] Once again men began to feel they were

1. Count Xavier de Maistre, 1754–1821, emigrated from his native country, Savoy, when this was conquered by the French in 1792; from 1802 on he represented his sovereign, the king of Sardinia, at the Court of Russia, where he wrote *Soirées de St. Pétersbourg;* having become a French subject in 1815, he wrote *Du pape* (1819), in which he expounded a

not free from the past, and their attitude toward it became again one of respect. But there was more in this than a return to the precedent-bound conservatism of pre-Enlightenment days: there was now the new concept of an organic unity embracing the whole of social life and linking the present generation by hidden bonds with its predecessors; the concept of a slow working of forces beyond the control of human will or reason—communal, anonymous forces which would not let themselves be denied or ignored, in which resided the reality of the destiny of nations or of mankind. In this concept was implied an acceptance of change, and to this extent it was not merely the conservatives who used the new vision of history to strengthen their position.[2]

---

counterrevolutionary system based on the supreme power of the Pope.

2. Thorbecke, for instance, the great Liberal statesman of Holland and author of the (virtually) new constitution of 1848—from which dates the whole movement of democratization that characterizes the ensuing period in Dutch history —laid stress on this aspect of the new historical theories he had become acquainted with in the 1820's while studying at German universities as the holder of a traveling scholarship. Before 1848 he was a professor of law at Leyden and in his writings proved himself to be a thinker and historian of unusual quality. It was in 1863 as prime minister, speaking in the Second Chamber, that he said: "He, it seems to me, has the true historical mind who knows how to appreciate each period in its own character and principle of development and to support the latter insofar as he is in a position to do so."

The significance for historical studies, at any rate, was great. Statesmen and prominent individuals generally were no longer envisaged simply as free agents, to be set up as examples or to be blamed and derided; rather were they thought of as the exponents of mysterious, organic social forces. These, too, historians told themselves, were not to be judged by the standards of the historian's own day; they were to be accepted, they were to be approached reverently. Indeed, the only way to establish contact with them was through the imagination, through sympathy, and what mattered was not the lesson that might be taught for the present day, still less the gratification of a contemporary feeling of superiority, but the revelation of this organic unity which was now felt to be the great treasure to be searched for in history.

The change was a momentous one for historical understanding. To prove it, at the beginning stands Herder, although long before him there had been the lonely Neapolitan thinker, Vico, so completely out of tune with his own time that his influence did not make itself fully felt until the early nineteenth

---

It is remarkable with what clearness of vision Thorbecke in an essay of 1844, "Over het hedendaagsch staatsburgerschap," *Historische Schetsen* (1860), anticipated the central thesis of Tocqueville's *L'ancien régime et la Révolution* (see above, p. 7): "The Revolution, in the matter of the building up of state power, beginning where the old practice had ended, completed a task which had long before been undertaken."

century.[3] But it was in Germany that the change was most conspicuously carried into effect. The names of Niebuhr,[4] Savigny,[5] and Ranke [6] will always be connected with the first triumphant examples of history written from the new point of view. Nowhere else after Vico did men like Goethe,[7] Schleiermacher,[8] and a host of others give so much thought to the wide philosophic implications of *Historismus*, the term which the Germans invented for this attitude. It is a term for which there is no generally accepted equivalent in English; I shall translate it "historism." The change has been described as the greatest contribution made by Germany to European civilization since the Reformation,[9] and indeed

3. Giambattista Vico, 1668–1744; his most famous work, *Scienza nuova*, appeared in 1725.

4. B. G. Niebuhr, 1776–1831; of Danish birth; Prussian ambassador to the Holy See 1816–23; after 1823 professor at Bonn. His pioneer *Römische Geschichte* appeared 1821–32.

5. K. F. von Savigny, 1779–1861; after some years of professorship at Berlin held high posts in the Prussian civil service. Through his work on the history of law he became the founder of the so-called Historic School of Law.

6. Leopold Ranke, 1795–1886; author of some fifty volumes, dealing mostly with German and European history of the sixteenth, seventeenth, and eighteenth centuries. See "Ranke in the Light of the Catastrophe" in my volume of essays *Debates with Historians*, The Hague, Nijhoff, 1955.

7. Johann Wolfgang Goethe, 1749–1832.

8. F. E. D. Schleiermacher, 1768–1834; theologian; after 1810 professor at the University of Berlin.

9. Friedrich Meinecke, *Die Entstehung des Historismus* (1936), *1, 2*.

the tendency or capacity to envisage the past in this way still forms part and parcel of our thinking. It still seems to us the historical outlook *par excellence;* compared with it we are inclined to regard the history of the seventeenth century and the Enlightenment as "unhistorical." The nineteenth century became the age of history. All study of the humanities, of language, literature, law, and religion was renewed by applying to it the historical method; by thinking about these subjects in terms of a process of growth and development; by trying, moreover, to refrain from measuring earlier ages by the reputedly stable, even eternal, standards of natural law—standards which were now dismissed as the projection of the living and judging generation's own particular civilization. The renewal of these studies came, on the contrary, by trying to enter into the habits of thought, sentiments, modes of behavior, and style of the period under review. An insight into the process of development, it was felt (and more so as the influence of science came to reinforce this tendency—I shall have something to say about Comte in a moment), opened up undreamed-of possibilities for a better understanding of contemporary conditions or phenomena. But apart from that, by the magic touch of sympathy civilization was enriched with a deeper knowledge of the phases of human existence, thought, or behavior, regarded no

32

longer as a collection of curiosities but as forms of life reanimated, integrated, significant for us in our own thinking and striving.

Is this, then, the use of history? It is one which I at any rate am fain to acknowledge gratefully. Yet it should not be thought that by means of this great discovery the old antithesis between use and abuse was disposed of. Far from it. A man like De Maistre, who was well aware of the new notions and could at times give eloquent expression to them, often in his use of history resembled a Voltaire of the Reaction, picking out from the storehouse of the past those incidents which seemed to support his preconceived conservative system. These new notions, in other words, did not provide a safeguard against the pressing of history into service for the counterrevolutionary outlook, somewhat in the way it had been made and by some was still being made to serve the cult of Reason.

Moreover, inherent in this new view was the possibility of an enslavement to history worse than that which prevailed in the centuries before the Enlightenment. Take Ranke, perhaps the sanest and most scholarly representative of the historical outlook of Romanticism. Patient and reverent toward the past, he drew treasure from it. What he set out to do, so he said in one of his earliest works, published in 1824, was not to judge the past but simply

33

to show how things had happened.[10] The historical process seemed to him the realization of God's plan. Humble and innocent-sounding phrases! But so averse did this attitude make him from applying moral standards to the deeds of the powerful actors of history, carried along, as he saw them, on the current of the prevailing Idea of their time, that it is often difficult to resist the impression that to him power is the unanswerable argument. What remains of the initiative or of the conscientious protest of the private individual? Is he not taught to find his salvation—and as Ranke does not shrink from saying, his freedom—in the awful decree of what actually comes to pass?

Yet there was in Ranke a humaneness and sensitivity by which the more rigorous implications of this philosophy are somehow softened. If these, nevertheless, appear so crudely in the writings of many of his followers, the circumstance is largely due to the combination of his influence with that of others, especially Hegel—an influence which sprang from another source altogether than the new Romanticism. Indeed, tendencies other than Romanticism survived and proved at times powerful in England, in France, even in Germany, and from these came uses of history in flagrant contradiction to the new spirit.

10. "Wie es eigentlich gewesen," *Geschichte der romanischen und germanischen Völkerschaften von 1494–1535.*

Hegel [11] was not a historian, he was a philosopher. He took up the idea of the historical process and hammered it into a system, and the result of this combination of history and philosophy proved an engine of dangerous potency in fitting men's minds for the struggles of politics.

Since Augustine there had been no such ambitions and impressive philosophy of history—I am not forgetting Bossuet or Vico—and no doubt Hegel owed to the *De civitate Dei* his basic idea of a *purposeful* development, a development that would bear out God's scheme. It is St. Augustine secularized, however; for Hegel, although he takes from the circumambient atmosphere of Romanticism the notion of organic unity within the orbit of the nation or state, is a child of the Enlightenment. He is imbued with its optimism, its belief in progress and perfectibility. And so history is to him the Absolute realizing itself, in periods and through peoples carefully noted, until complete freedom has been attained through *understanding*—that is, through his own philosophy, finest flower of the choice product of that cosmic process—the monarchical and Lutheran Prussian state.

11. G. W. F. Hegel, 1770–1831; from 1818 professor of philosophy in Berlin. His views on history are scattered over the whole of his extensive works; the *Philosophie der Geschichte*, in which they were systematically expounded, was published posthumously in 1837, based on his notes for academic lectures.

It seems to me so obvious as hardly to require stating, but let me say it in unmistakable terms: these large systems in which history is made to go through a course of so many stages to some end either of salvation or perdition are not based on observation of the facts of history. They do not spring from history, they are imposed upon it. They spring from the philosopher's or the prophet's mind, dominated by the enthusiasm of faith (or it may be—as was the case with Spengler,[12] the prophet of doom—by despair at the lack of faith). I seem to see these system builders exulting, joyfully or gloomily, at the spectacle of the world and its bewildering past, of all great happenings, of nations, kings, and centuries, obediently falling into a pattern at the behest of *their* imagination and ingenuity and to the greater glory of *their* principle. St. Augustine comforting himself in the dire anxieties of his time with the thought that the wicked in their triumph are the means by which God works to the predestined end of the salvation of the elect (of whom he is one); Hegel singing his paean to the Cosmic Spirit, the incarnation of Reason, which, cunningly making use of even the passions and crimes of the unenlightened, advances through phase upon phase of history

12. Oswald Spengler, 1880–1936; author of *Der Untergang des Abendlandes*, 1919. The title of the English translation, *The Decline of the West*, unduly weakens the force of the word *Untergang:* "doom" or "ruin" would be better.

36

toward the consummation of complete freedom (toward, in other words, the Prussia of his day and toward his philosophy, in which the Cosmic Spirit looks back upon the process of its own objectivization)—I can't help being struck by the gigantic presumption and by the gigantic egotism. I can conceive no more flagrant contradiction to the genuine version of the historical attitude of mind that sprang from German Romanticism, the attitude Ranke formulated in that famous phrase about every epoch being immediate to God. "Its value," he went on, "consists not at all in what springs from it but in its own existence, its own self." Hegel was interested in past epochs only insofar as they lent themselves to his manipulations for the arrangement of a process of which he and his Prussia were the outcome.

Yet, presumptuous and egocentric as was Hegel's system and composed, moreover, of warring elements, Romantic and Enlightened, it made an enormous impression. Indeed, the attempt at a synthesis between these two forces, both rooted in the fundamental aspirations of humanity, no doubt counted for much among the reasons for its success. It must be admitted, too, that the encyclopedic comprehensiveness and the subtlety of phrasing and argument *are* impressive, and to have provided generations with a method for ordering their thoughts (so much so that even minds impervious to the fascination had to account to the world or to themselves their reasons for rejecting the system) is no mean feat. In any case, however fanciful these systems may be—I am thinking here not of Hegel only— through the impact they have on other minds, their disciples', even their most hostile critics', they do achieve an undeniable reality.

As for Hegel, the tendency of his philosophy as he presented it was strongly conservative. Rationalism was hitched to the wagon of Prussian monarchy, the state generally, or all constituted power. "Whatever is rational, *is;* and whatever *is,* is rational." This phrase, indeed the whole system, could be used and was used to defend existing conditions; but it proved easy to make them serve very different purposes. A man like Marx, whose heart was set upon change, reform, revolution managed to make the Cosmic Spirit work history for *his* end and succeeded in appropriating the crushing self-confidence of Hegel's thought for the purposes of a dynamic instead of a static or conservative policy.

This, after all, was the fundamental characteristic of Hegel's immense intellectual effort—that he, pretending to identify himself with the historic process and the Cosmic Spirit, in fact subjected both to his philosophy or conservative faith. In this, in the feeling that by understanding the cosmic process one has become its master—in the resulting conviction that one's particular beliefs have the sanction of destiny and are invincible—lies the chief attraction which the system has exercised, and through some of its later adaptations still exercises, on so many minds.

Abuse of history with a vengeance! But history could be, and was, abused without the aid of Hegel. Carlyle, Michelet, Macaulay [13]—of these three only Carlyle had more than a superficial knowledge of Hegel, and what influenced him much more in his German readings were the true Romantic notions of organic unity and the insufficiency of human reason. Now observe how he applied them in a way strikingly divergent from Ranke's, consigning whole centuries to Satan and Nothingness, letting God (or the Eternal, the Unknowable) rule by thunder and lightning. These prophetic and apocalyptic peculiarities, which occasionally no doubt have their own impressiveness, spring from extraneous elements, from the remnants of Carlyle's Calvinistic upbringing and from his temperament. In spite of them the new historic feeling enabled him to write history which at times communicates to the reader the most acute, the most moving sense of contact with the reality of the past, but at the same time his

13. In addition to the one on Ranke, essays on Carlyle (1795–1881), Macaulay (1800–59), and Michelet (1798–1874) will be found in *Debates with Historians*, 1955. Carlyle's *French Revolution* appeared in 1837, Michelet's *Histoire de la Révolution française* in 1847–53; new ed. Gerard Walter in Bibliothèque de la Pléiade. Macaulay began publishing essays in 1824; the first volume of his *History of England* appeared in 1850.

Romantic notions lured him into a more naked idolatry of power than Ranke was ever guilty of. In his *French Revolution* they blinded Carlyle to all save the destructive tendencies of that immense event, so much did the close connection of its positive side with rationalism arouse his scorn.

It will give an idea of the diversity of the uses to which history can be put if we now turn to Michelet's *History of the French Revolution*, which appeared only a few years after Carlyle's. At the outset of his academic career Michelet had paid homage to the new German notion that the historian must enter into the thoughts of every saint and heresiarch and do justice to every cause and every period according to its own light. In the forties of the century, however, he renounced these ideas once and for all.

Carried away by the wave of anticlericalism and revolutionary ardor that was sweeping France, he rushed headlong into a glorification of the French Revolution as the beginning of the reign of Justice and Liberty. Nothing more directly opposed to the view taken by that other Romantic emotionalist, Carlyle, could well be imagined—nor anything less historical in the German sense—than when Michelet now proclaims the spirit of the Revolution to be his sole adviser in judging (and condemning wholesale) the preceding ages. Michelet did not need Hegel to teach anything on the score of confidence or of thinking in absolutes, for indeed he was indebted for those essentially unhistorical mental attitudes to another philosopher: Rousseau.

Michelet and Carlyle, in spite of the contrast presented by their interpretations of the Revolution, were in temperament and intellectual structure not unlike. Totally different, on the contrary, was Macaulay, their contemporary. Completely untouched by Romanticism, he wrote as the cerebral, argumentative, lawyer-like advocate of progress, the herald of the triumphs of liberalism and enlightenment. The past was severely questioned on what it had contributed to the good cause, and of all who had ever offered it resistance Macaulay spoke in the most indignant or coldly contemptuous terms. Carlyle and he were at opposite poles in their outlook upon the world and upon history; from Michelet, too, he differed sharply, for liberty and justice had not, in his opinion, been discovered in 1789, or in France. But however different the cause he serves, it is in that service that he compels history to perform, and his cause, too, inspires him to dispose of the past with a certitude and confidence, different in quality but equal in strength.

Hegel's influence was most directly felt in Germany. He was behind the writers of the so-called Prussian school, behind Droysen and Sybel and the brilliant Treitschke,[14] who in the fifties and sixties arranged German history so as to bring out Prussia's mission as the agent of German unity, and when unity had been established in 1870 continued to use that scheme of a natural and rational course of events culminating in glorious and inevitable consummation. Meanwhile, as I have hinted, Marx [15] had adapted Hegel's system. Instead of representing history as the process of Absolute Thought thinking itself into reality, he introduced his materialistic conception of the dominating part played by economic relationships. But he retained the dynamic interpretation of history as a movement in determined stages toward an end of universal bliss, stages and end foreseen by him and announced with all the fervor of an apostle chosen for a divine revelation. The authority he arrogated to himself, the authority which was to impress successive generations

14. J. G. Droysen, 1808–84; after 1859 professor at the University of Berlin; his *Geschichte der preussischen Politik* began to appear in 1855. H. Sybel, 1817–95; professor in Munich and Bonn, repeatedly member of the Prussian House of Representatives; his *Begründung des deutschen Kaiserreiches durch Wilhelm I* belongs to the last period of his life. H. von Treitschke, 1834–96; originally a Saxon, after 1874 professor at the University of Berlin; from 1871 member of the German Diet. *Historisch-politische Aufsätze*, 1865; his uncompleted *Deutsche Geschichte im 19. Jahrhundert* began to appear in 1879.

15. Karl Marx, 1818–83. The Communist Manifesto dates from 1847, the first edition of *Das Kapital* from 1867.

of his followers, was that of science—scientific observation of social phenomena. Yet both he and Treitschke, in their very different causes, took from Hegel that philosophic panoply (first forged, it should not be forgotten, in the powerful imagination of Augustine) which protected them from any doubts when invoking history as their omnipotent ally, history interpreted so as to suit their passionate politics. "Who can be so blind," exclaimed Treitschke at the moment of witnessing the triumph of 1870, "as to deny that in the wonderful happenings of these days works the divine Intelligence that compels us Germans to become a nation?"

The great moment inevitably creates the men of strong arms and eloquent lips needed for victory, and even the enemy is forced (by that cunning of the Idea, of which Hegel spoke) to serve it. Thus, Marx is convinced that capitalism will dig its own grave. It had been to Rousseau's concept of the general will (which might not be the will of the majority but which was Reason itself and could not err) that Robespierre owed his fanatical determination to found the Republic of Virtue by exterminating its enemies. Marx, forecasting a dictatorship of the proletariat as an indispensable final stage before the attainment of complete economic and consequently spiritual freedom, justified it as willed by History.

History, that is, which was Reason in action. In the end, if we compare the Reign of Terror in

France and the lasting influence which the revolutionary mentality has had in that country with the fortunes of nationalist fanaticism in Germany and of Marxist fanaticism as it ultimately, through Lenin and Stalin, came to make its home in Russia, Reason seems to have reinforced itself with History only to arrive at similar results. So much at any rate has become clear that the new approach to history, inaugurated in reaction to the unhistorical Enlightenment, fruitful and salutary as it has proved to be, does not by itself rule out the exploitation of the past for the wildest and most pernicious purposes. Indeed, if the nineteenth century may be called the age of history, it is also the age in which history has been made as shamelessly to serve reaction or revolution—in fact every party and every power—as in any period of which I know.

But I have been dealing with the excesses. The main stream of historical thought and historical writing was less torrential, although certainly not without dangers of its own. I am not thinking of the theological interpretation of history, which survived all changes and transformations of historical thought. It can now best be described as a backwater.[16] The

16. Clergymen of all churches, in times of national jubilation or sorrow, presume to explain the cause of events by confident assertions about the divine will. I wrote an essay last year on the celebration in 1863 of the liberation of Holland in 1813 ("1813 gevierd in 1863," *De Gids*, 1954) and gave some striking instances of this theological interpretation of

main stream of thought, from the middle of the nineteenth century, perhaps has been more deeply influenced by Comte than by Hegel. Comte, the father of Positivism, had his own system of historical development, in so many stages, a system founded more exclusively than that of Hegel on science.[17] The scientific method applied to history—this is his great contribution. "History," he wrote, with the confidence characteristic of so many philosophers, "has now been for the first time systematically considered as a whole [by him, Comte] and has been found, like other phenomena, subject to invariable laws."

The great task before the historian, he thought, must henceforth be to discover those laws. Given the

the great event in particular and of Dutch history in general from sermons, pamphlets, and poems. René Rémond notices the same phenomenon occurring in France after the disaster of 1870–71 (*La Droite en France de 1815 à nos jours*, 1954, p. 132): "A des esprits familiarisés avec l'analogie scolastique, exercés à déchiffrer le sens spirituel des textes sacrés, il apparaît naturel de chercher le sens caché que tout événement porte en lui, hors de ses causes visibles. Les voilà donc qui vont scruter les circonstances et faire parler l'histoire, au nom d'un concordisme assez élémentaire. . . . [There had been miraculous warnings, la Salette, Lourdes, Pont-main.] Restée sourde à ces objurgations, la France a été justement châtiée de son endurcissement."

17. Auguste Comte, 1798–1857; founder of the science of sociology and of the positivist system of philosophy. His *Système de politique positive ou traité de sociologie, instituant la religion de l'humanité* appeared 1851–54.

ever increasing prestige of science as the nineteenth
century saw it advance from one great victory to
another, historians must be tempted to tackle the
job. To talk the language of science, to pride themselves on having applied its methods, became a habit
with historians. The concepts of Darwin, for instance, intended for biology, were eagerly annexed
for history. Marxism sailed merrily along on this
same current. A pure Positivist of Comte's school,
Buckle, wrote the ambitious *History of Civilization
in England*, which purported to show the laws by
which the progress of civilization toward ever more
complete enlightenment is governed.[18] Buckle is
now forgotten, but there was Taine, one of the most
brilliant minds among historical writers in the second
half of the century.[19] In Taine's system the influence
of Comte predominates, although fused with that of
Hegel. He solemnly declared history to be dominated by the three factors of race, surroundings, and
moment, a formula which has a fine scientific ring
about it but which can be handled in almost any case

18. Henry Thomas Buckle, 1821–62; *History of Civilization
in England*, 1857.

19. Hippolyte Taine, 1828–93; philosopher, historian, and
literary historian. The quotations below, in the text, are taken
respectively from *La Fontaine et ses fables*, 1853; *Histoire de
la littérature anglaise*, 1863; *Les Origines de la France con-
temporaine*, Pt. 1 *L'Ancien Régime* (1875), and Vol. 3 of Pt. 2
La Révolution, 1885; *Histoire de la littérature anglaise*; and
a letter to Havet, Nov. 18, 1885, quoted by G. Monod, *Renan,
Taine, Michelet*, p. 127.

with the most widely different results. In successive prefaces he asserted that man is an animal of a superior kind which produces philosophies more or less as silkworms make cocoons; that vice and virtue are products in the same way that vitriol or sugar are; that he regarded his subject, the transformation of French civilization in the course of the eighteenth century, with the eyes of a natural scientist observing the metamorphosis of an insect; while he presented his volume on the Reign of Terror as a treatise on "moral zoology." Renaissance, Classicism, Alexandrine, or Christian epoch—"there is here, as everywhere, nothing but a problem of mechanics." "What matters is," he wrote in a private letter twenty years after that statement, "a scientific opinion. My impressions don't count. What I want is to collaborate in a system of research which will in fifty years' time permit honest men to have something better than sentimental or egoistic impressions about the public affairs of their own day."

The fifty years have long passed (the letter was written in 1885), but although the mass of well-established facts relating to innumerable aspects of the past has constantly grown, and although the severest methods of sifting and testing, comparing and combining have been and are still being applied —although, in short, we historians have done and are still doing our best—few of us will nowadays maintain that the day is near when sentiment or egoism can be eliminated from the interpretation or presentation of the past.

The provocative crudity with which Taine expressed himself in these prefaces, and the glaring contradiction presented by the highly sensitive and personal quality, even violent partisanship, of the books they introduced to the public alienated many of his contemporaries. There was particularly Sainte-Beuve,[20] who at the heyday of philosophic or systematized or symbolic history was in the habit of making comments of astringent and wholesome skepticism, to the effect that the individuality of the actor and the uniqueness of the event in history should not be forgotten, that the observer should humbly remember his human quality and not pretend to be in control of the fortuitous and the unforeseeable.

Today, at any rate, most of us know that it is not so simple. Large regions of history have no doubt proved suitable for methods of research which may be called scientific. Collaboration of historical scholars can yield valuable results. Notwithstanding, or rather for the very reason of, our half century more of experience, we know that history will not so readily give up her secret at the bidding of the

20. Charles Augustin Sainte-Beuve, literary critic and historian, 1804–69. Cf. Charly Guyot, *Sainte-Beuve et les philosophes de l'histoire.*

magic word "science." We have grown somewhat wary of this scientific terminology applied to history. The view of history as an organic development has proved extraordinarily fertile, it is still helpful, but it should not be thought that the word "organism" in its biological sense can represent a historical reality. It is no more than a metaphor; it is a token used for a working method. In Taine's own day, however, the spirit animating professions of faith such as the ones quoted exercised an influence not often leading to unconditional acceptance but so extensive as to set a mark on the period, and this for the whole of the Western world. And as a matter of fact, that spirit has by no means been cast out, nor has the mark been effaced.

It is a curious thing to observe the combinations that proved possible. There is little to surprise in the mingling of deterministic Marxism with Comtist Positivism, out to establish the laws of social life. But just as Romanticism and Hegelianism, in many ways opposed, were nevertheless able at times to support each other, so even Positivism and the Romantic tradition—than which no two attitudes of mind seem at first sight to have less affinity—could meet in certain minds to reinforce a particular tendency in the approach to the past. I mean the tendency already pointed out in Ranke. Ranke never surrendered to Hegel and his irresistible Absolute unfolding itself and using men as tools to advance its ends. Also, when he was well past middle age, he was moved to a, for him, most unusual outburst of anger at the claim of the Positivist School to cast the development which to him seemed a play of moral forces directed by God into the iron bondage of unfeeling laws of nature. Yet Ranke, in his admiration before the divine disposal of human affairs, was very loath to criticize the actions of historical characters, and power or success especially seemed to reduce his moral judgment to silence. But did not the Hegelian and the Positivist views of history have the same effect? The man to be praised, according to Marx, is the man who swims with the tide of history. The attitude of the historian, says Taine, should be the attitude of the natural scientist. Is the natural scientist moved to indignation by the habits of the poison snake? Does the pig rouse in him feelings of disgust?

So both Hegelianism and Positivism strengthened a tendency already present in historism as a possibility, one which, carried to excess, gave to the word the pejorative meaning it is often felt to convey. I have mentioned a number of nineteenth-century historians who, either untouched by historism, like Macaulay, or in revolt against it, like Michelet and the Prussian nationalists, took violent sides in the struggles of the past, condemning or ridiculing from the point of view of a system really rooted in their own time; and I have not concealed my opinion that this does not seem to me the true historical approach. However, when I acknowledge my belief in historism as the true way of looking at the past, the way in accordance with the best and most rewarding tendencies of modern civilization, it does not mean—and I hinted as much before—that I overlook the peculiar pitfalls which it presents.

Historism may lead the historian to surrender his own standard of values, almost his own personality, and to dissolve into the past or into the historical process. Seeing every conception and every ideal as the result of a development which will continue after his own day and is bound further to transform them, he may come to doubt the existence of any stable value outside the impersonal stream of events, and his opinions will float along with it. Not only will he shrink from criticism of historical personages and from expressions of admiration as well (waves, or wavelets, spray, driven before the gale), but any kind of independence with regard to the historical process will become impossible to him; the relationship between past and present will seem to him above all to inculcate submission. Unless the historical process is reduced to some rigid system! In that case the feeling of floating along may yield to one of being supported or driven, and an inhuman and amoral energy be imparted. Generally, however, with that important and no less deplorable exception, the result will be a boundless relativism, an impotence to assert individualism or opposition; patience, tolerance, acceptance will become the only virtues.

It is against this state of mind particularly that Nietzsche, in 1874, uttered his impassioned protest in the essay "About the Usefulness and Harmfulness of History." [21] History, according to him, was becoming a drag on the movement of the human spirit, a menace to the freedom of man's soul. History stood in the way of life. He scoffed at Hegel, for whom "the culminating and final point of the cosmic process coincided with his own Berlin existence." Hegel had not actually said that everything coming after him would be superfluous, but he *had* "planted in the generations fertilized by his influence that admiration for *the power of history* which will at all moments virtually turn into naked admiration for success and into idolization of the actual state of affairs." Similarly, Nietzsche girded at Comte (though without mentioning him by name) and the pretense that history should be a science. Everything reduced to the movements of masses and brought under the dominance of laws! As if the real tenor of history were not: "Once there was . . ." and as if

21. Friedrich Nietzsche, 1844–1900; from 1869 to 1879 professor in classical philology at the University of Basel in Switzerland. His *Unzeitgemässe Betrachtungen*, of which the essay *Vom Nutzen und Nachtheil der Historie für das Leben* is one, appeared 1873–76.

morality did not command: "Thou shalt not," or "thou shouldst not have." "To take everything objectively, neither to hate nor to love anything, to understand it all—how soft and pliant will that make a man!"

No, deeds done in despite of the blind power of facts, in despite of the tyranny of actuality—this is what matters.[22]

Splendid pages are these in Nietzsche's little book. for one cannot read this vindication, against the overstrained claims of history, of the rights of spontaneity and initiative, of individualism and personal greatness without feeling a glow of gratitude and sympathy. One German scholar had been preaching "the complete surrender of the personality to the cosmic process." With withering sarcasm Nietzsche exclaims: "The personality and the cosmic process! The cosmic process and the personality of the flea beetle! If only these gentry would not talk forever, in their hyperbolic fashion, of the Cosmos, Cosmos, Cosmos! The only honest mode of speech would be to let us hear about men, men, men!"

But although Nietzsche may be among the most stimulating of writers, he is the unsafest and most erratic guide imaginable. His reminder that life must

22. The passages quoted will be found in the separate edition of *Vom Nutzen und Nachteil* (spelling modernized) in the Sammlung Birkhäuser, Basel, no year given (*ca.* 1950), on pp. 78, 79, 80, 83, 66, 91.

not allow itself to be imprisoned by history, his insistence that history only shows us men, men struggling with blind forces—I should like to extract those passages from the famous essay and have every historian read them at least once every year of his life. But side by side with these inspiring remarks are others in which the claims of life are overstrained no less than had ever been those of history by the historists. And it is this unmeasured exaltation of life—that is, to him, of instinct, passion, courage, self—which has proved Nietzsche's great and insidious attraction. He has been, and still is, the favorite of revolutionists and rebels, of some who have proved their demonic conception of life in the awful reality of twentieth-century politics, and of others who have merely been at loggerheads with society to the extent of writing clever books bristling with impatience and irritation at every restraint of sanity, at balance and compromise, seeking freedom and a sense of power in their literary triumphs over what they have been pleased to call Philistinism or dry-as-dust scholarship. Not historism but history itself is to Nietzsche and his followers the enemy—unless they can make her their slave.

For, says Nietzsche, what man needs in order to do great things, what peoples need in order to ripen, is the sheltering cloud of illusion, and it is this that history as now practiced is out to dispel. What has been left of Christianity since the historical method

set to work upon it? It has become listless and un-
natural, it has been dissolved into mere knowledge
about Christianity and so destroyed. These doctrines
about the sovereign power of development, of the
changing nature of all conceptions, types, and modes
may be true—nay, Nietzsche says expressly that he
does believe them to be true, "true but fatal." To
keep on instilling them into people's minds will end
in the people being ruined in the pursuit of miserable
petty interests and ceasing to be a people. So Nietzsche, here and in much of his later work even more
ecstatically, praised the myth as needful for great
and fruitful living, and not the least object of his
essay is to call off history from the tracking down of
myths with relentless, truth-seeking criticism and
turn her into the unscrupulous bodyguard of his
adventurous Life Force.

Nietzsche would no doubt have despised the
Houston Stewart Chamberlains [23] and the Rosen-
bergs and the other prophets of National Socialism;
he would soon have rebelled against Mussolini and
Hitler, had he lived to know them. But these modern
enthusiasts for the sovereign rights of instinct and

23. Houston Stewart Chamberlain, 1855–1927; his *Grund-
lagen des neunzehnten Jahrhunderts* (1899) is based on the
idea of the superiority of the Germanic race; Alfred Rosen-
berg (1893–1946) can be described as a disciple of H. S. C.;
he stressed the antisemitic tendency and in his *Der Mythus
des 20. Jahrhunderts* gave the most widely read philosophy of
National Socialism.

passion, these cultivators of the useful myth, have nevertheless given the world a terrible object lesson on where history can land us when it is detached from criticism and truth and made to serve the uninhibited ambitions of emotionalists.

It is curious to observe, once again, how Nietzsche, in this matter of the terrible abuse of history characteristic of the twentieth century, has in effect become the ally of Hegel, whom he so cordially detested. For in the totalitarian system of Communism, which owes a primary debt to Hegel, the teaching of Nietzsche that history will be destructive unless she be made to help the myth and even to help in building it up can be watched as in a mirror of practice; a distorting mirror it may be, but one which brings out certain features with all the more devastating clearness.

I need hardly say that Nietzsche did not discover the usefulness of the myth; but rarely had it been proclaimed with such blatant frankness. Nor are the totalitarian regimes of our time the first to show themselves impressed with the idea. Almost every established power, every state and every church, every party, group, and dynasty has always regarded with suspicion the true historian approaching its past with fearless criticism. Its past seems to each to have importance for the present. I have mentioned how this conviction dominated party warfare in the seventeenth century, but it is a conviction of all ages and by no means extinct today.

Yet hardly ever has a government proceeded so systematically as the Soviet government is doing to-day in fashioning its own myth and in drilling the historians to support it. The unfortunate Russian historians, if they value their lives, will carefully refrain from expressing any doubts which may occur to them privately. The elimination of Trotski [24] from the official history of the 1917 Revolution, the prominence given in it to Stalin, who was at that time really a character of secondary importance; the actual scrapping from the big Soviet encyclopedia of the pages in which the life of Beria [25] was recorded —these are instances that will occur to many readers, for in the Western world they have attracted a good deal of attention and caused surprise, ridicule, indignation.

Indeed, although these excesses may be the out-come of a tendency which is universal in time and place, it is a fact that there is a long-standing tradition in our Western civilization, a tradition which

24. Trotski (Leib Bronstein), 1879–1940. After playing a most important part in the Bolshevist revolution Trotski, in 1928, was exiled on account of his opposition to Stalin.
25. L. P. Beria (1899–1953), a leading member of the Soviet inner circle, was arrested in July, 1953, following hard upon the death of Stalin, March 5; Beria was executed on Dec. 23.

has for generations now been growing stronger, of respect for the right of history to untrammeled investigation and criticism. We have a fundamental contrast here between the ways of thinking in the democratic and in the totalitarian world, and at the same time an indication of the importance of history —history free from system and bias, as a distinctive and vital element of our civilization.

I have had so much to say on the abuses of history that the whole trend of my argument may at times have seemed somewhat depressingly negative. At least I have been able to end this chapter on a more positive note, and if I have not done more now than just lightly touch that chord, there still remain reflections to be put forward which I trust will restore the balance.

CHAPTER THREE

*W*E HAVE SEEN how roughly some of the great historians of the nineteenth century, emboldened by philosophies of varied origins, handled the patient and forever silent material of the past. They forced it into strikingly expressive shapes which are often intensely moving or inspiring; but when the collection is viewed as a whole, what disconcerts the beholder is the lack of unity, since all these works respond to the fiercely held but mutually hostile convictions of their respective authors.

In the past generation or two the situation of history has changed in that the position of the professional, academic historian has become stronger. To the detriment, it is often said, of the popularity of history and of its ability to perform its proper social function. The plodding, unimaginative expert, writer of monographs which only his fellow workers in the field will read (to pick holes in them most likely), piling up knowledge which is of no interest

to the world at large—everybody knows the un
attractive picture. It has been the theme of a thou
sand denunciations, in tone varying from bored
contempt to scathing sarcasm or vehement indignation. The picture is a caricature. No doubt there is
a very great deal of work done that must necessarily
remain within the small circle of men devoting their
lives to allied studies, but it should not be forgotten
that such work is an indispensable preliminary to the
large syntheses which can reach a wider circle of
readers, or that the unambitious, devoted worker
can through his specialized pursuits attain to com-
munion with the true historic spirit no less, very
often even better, than the brilliant writer using the
other man's results for a more comprehensive purpose.

One thing, however, must be admitted. The great
writers of history, outstanding in the literature and
general civilization of their day, as in their different
ways were Carlyle and Macaulay, Ranke and
Treitschke, Michelet and Taine, have become very
rare. Specialization and the emphasis on technical
exactitude are proving an embarrassment to the free
use of the imagination. Undeniably, the imagination
has a great part to play if history is to evoke or interpret the past significantly. How freely it should be
allowed to act does of course remain the question.

This much is certain: the quality which the
academic and specialized study of history tends to

develop is that of caution. Much might be said concerning the effects of that quality. I shall be the
first to agree when it is urged that they are not always admirable. But from the welter of apprecia-
tions, favorable and unfavorable, that will here
present themselves to the mind, there is one which
must be discussed because it concerns the general
view of what history can and cannot do.

The prevailing mood among professional historians nowadays is a chastened one in the face of
the immense mass of material and the infinite complexity of the phenomena. Not a new feeling certainly: I noticed it above in Sainte-Beuve. Nowadays, at all events, the great majority of working
historians are aware that certainty in history is beyond the grasp of the human mind. Not only is the
multitude of facts staggering, but their nature is
acknowledged to be elusive. The fact in history cannot be isolated. In itself it is meaningless; it can be
made to show different aspects of meaning only as it
is related to different parts of the circumstances in
which it is embedded. Causation, too, is not the simple affair which historians of an earlier generation
often thought it to be. Hardly ever, and less so as
the questions at issue become larger and more complicated, can one factor be confidently picked out
as having caused an event or set in movement a train
of events. Complicated situations have to be taken
into account; many factors will be seen to have had

an influence, directly or remotely. What makes it particularly difficult to strike a balance between the respective effects of the factors governing a given situation is that they will often be dissimilar in nature: the acts of an individual, the inarticulate feeling of a crowd, military defeat or victory, economic desires or distress, religious fervor. In deciding upon the particular aspect of a fact or upon the proportionate importance to be assigned to a number of factors, the historian must be guided to some extent if not by his prejudice or predilection at any rate by his point of view and intention, determined by the delimitation implied in his subject. An awareness of this predicament was strikingly expressed by Maitland, that illustrious specialist, over half a century ago: "Such is the unity of all history that anyone who endeavors to tell a piece of it must feel that his first sentence tears a seamless web." [1]

But the historian cannot evade his responsibility. To ascertain the bare facts or factors, sometimes a difficult job in all conscience, is only the first stage of his work: if he is to give an intelligible account, if he will to his own satisfaction *understand*, he must use his material by choosing from it, ordering it, and interpreting it. In doing so he is bound to introduce an element of subjectivity; that is, he will tamper

1. F. W. Maitland, 1850–1906; from 1888 professor at Cambridge University. His *History of English Law before the Time of Edward I* appeared in 1895.

with or detract from the absolute, unchanging truth. "I shall stick to the facts," "I shall let the facts speak for themselves"—these well-known turns of speech are often permissible enough, but they are apt to be as misleading as that other favorite phrase: "History shows." Behind the facts, behind the goddess History, there is a historian. Clio may be in possession of the truth, the whole truth, and nothing but the truth, but to the historian (the young, middle-aged, or old lady or gentleman rummaging among papers in the archive or writing at a desk) she will at best, in exchange for their labor and devotion, vouchsafe a glimpse. Never will she surrender the whole of her treasure. The most that we can hope for is a partial rendering, an approximation, of the real truth about the past.

What I have been saying is no more than a commonplace of current historical thought. But the profound truth of it was borne in upon me—I said at the outset that I was going to write from my own experience—when during the years of the German occupation of Holland I examined the French historiography on Napoleon. Nothing struck me so forcibly, while reading one brilliant French writer after another—and in fact it was the same story with the less brilliant ones, and the sober academic historians of the last period were not, for all their caution exempt from the general law—nothing struck me so much as to find how the point of view of each, conditioned by the political circumstances and preoccupations of his own day, had influenced his judgment and appreciation of the great man. Napoleon could be seen either as the son or as the tamer of the Revolution, either as the bearer of the glad tidings of emancipation to the nations of Europe or as their oppressor, either as the great warrior defending France against a coalition of bigoted and envious European powers or as the adventurer thirsting after personal glory and dragging France along on a path of idle victories inevitably ending in disaster. It was possible to distinguish successive waves of admiration and detraction, of for and against: *for*, when Frenchmen were suffering from a sense of humiliation or of boredom under the restored Bourbons and Louis Philippe; *against*, when in Napoleon III they saw the imperial despotism revived and did not like it; *for*, once again, when the scandals and distractions of the Third Republic began to disgust them with parliamentary government.

Are not these findings somewhat discouraging as to the value of history? Some have been discouraged; some have ignored the verdict; others have looked for ways out, refusing to accept it.

The young historian in Sartre's [2] novel *La Nausée* reflects: "The present is what exists, and all that is not present does not exist. The past does not exist."

2. Jean Paul Sartre, *b.* 1905; the philosopher of existentialism.

Overwhelmed with a feeling of disgust, he cannot continue writing his book. Before Sartre, Valéry, engrossed in the contemplation of the Eternal Present, never tired of gibing at the impotence of history.[3]

The system builders, on the other hand, are not to be denied. The worst of Toynbee's great attempt is that he has presented it under the patronage of a scientific terminology.[4] A patently aprioristically conceived, Augustinian-Spenglerian scheme of the history of mankind he wants to pass off as the product of the empirical method, built up out of what he calls facts, without troubling to analyze their precise

3. Paul Valéry, 1871–1945; French poet and thinker. Valéry's hostility to history was not an absolute one. It was directed rather against history as practiced by the historians. At times he mentioned criteria with the help of which valuable history might be written; if only his advice were followed, historians might improve their discipline and their methods and history more nearly approach to being a science. See Maurice Bémol, *Paul Valéry* (1949), p. 171. To the historian, however, his directions are likely to appear arbitrary, the outcome of a purely personal aversion to the contradictoriness and particularity of life and hankering after the absolute.

4. Arnold J. Toynbee, *b.* 1888; professor in the University of London, Director of the Royal Institute of International Affairs, author of *A Study of History*, 10 vols. 1934–54. I have repeatedly written about the great work and attempted to show in detail the hollowness to its pretense of being based on empiricism and logical induction. The four essays I devoted to it between 1946 and 1955 may now be found in *Debates with Historians*.

nature or test their reliability for the purposes of system construction. When in a radio debate with him nearly seven years ago I remarked upon the bewildering multiplicity as well as baffling intangibility of historical data, he asked: "Is history really too hard a nut for science to crack?" and added: " 'The human intellect,' sighs Geyl, 'is not sufficiently comprehensive.' " Of course I had not sighed; why should I sigh about what I regard as one of the fundamental truths of life? But Toynbee's rejoinder was: "We can't afford such defeatism, it is unworthy of the greatness of man's mind." [5] In short, he belongs to those who obstinately blind themselves to the limitations of our comprehension of history.

I shall not dispute that the vision of history in the four final volumes of his immense work which he has now completed has grandeur. It is not, however, history that has dictated to him this vision but his passion for unity, a passion fundamentally antagonistic to history, the guardian of the particular. Of all the passions, is there one more merciless and

5. The debate was published separately in *Can we Know the Pattern of the Past? Discussion between P. Geyl and A. J. Toynbee;* Bussum, the Netherlands, Kroonders, 1948; reprinted with my first set criticism of *A Study of History* ("Toynbee's System of Civilizations," now also to be found in *Debates with Historians*) and an essay on Toynbee by Professor Sorokin, in *The Pattern of the Past*, Boston, Mass., Beacon Press, 1949.

devouring? Even when, as here, it is decked out with the language of the religion of love, and even though, I have no doubt, it is inspired by the fear of mankind destroying itself unless restrained by some new spiritual and political orientation, I cannot help seeing in the passion for unity a Moloch which in its own way presents mankind, whose very life is diversity, with a new and deadly danger.

More subtle, though at the same time less impressive, is Romein, the Amsterdam Professor of History, who is at home the leading representative of a system of thought against which I have more than once felt irresistibly urged to enter the field.[6] Romein begins by admitting the difficulty: our comprehension of history *is* subject to limitations. But in his craving for certainty he has in his neo-Marxian philosophy found that useful ally, the *Zeitgeist*. Curiously enough, Romein has been unable to resist the fascination of Toynbee, the prophet of Christianity; he has fallen for that glorious conception of the unity of mankind; "universalist solidarity," as the philosopher of that Amsterdam School, Romein's friend Pos, has dubbed it, easily divesting it of its Christian garb and retaining the stark reality of one way of life enforced by one authority.[7] But it is

6. Jan Romein, *b.* 1894; professor at the University of Amsterdam since 1939.

7. H. J. Pos, *b.* 1898; professor at the University of Amsterdam since 1932, after holding for some years a chair in the Free (Calvinistic) University in the town.

especially with the magic assistance of the Zeitgeist that Romein manages to escape from the implications of his admission of our limitations.

Provided that the historian, he asserts, is in harmony with the spirit of his own time (but it has to be the true spirit of the time), he may rest assured that he can attain certainty about the past. This objectivation of subjectivity is indeed a remarkable conjuring trick. But I need only recall what was said in the preceding chapter about Hegel to make it clear that there is nothing novel in this attempt of a historian to divest himself of his personal responsibility in order to evoke the awful majesty emanating from that mysterious (but in fact self-created) divinity.

More openly subjectivistic is the theory of the German philosopher Theodore Lessing, whose book *History as Giving Sense to the Senseless* made quite a stir shortly after the first World War.[8] In a remarkably eloquent and at times extraordinarily acute argument, making use of all the new psychological theories of the subconscious and the philosophical refinements of the limitations of man's capacity for knowing reality, he accepted the verdict of guilty and proceeded triumphantly to pass sentence of death on historical scholarship and criticism. "History needs and employs the statement 'This or that

8. Theodor Lessing, 1872–1933; his *Geschichte als Sinngebung des Sinnlosen* appeared in 1919.

happened then and there' for no other purpose than to transform mere happening into the poetry of significant destiny." "To know scientifically is to destroy illusion; Clio on the contrary builds up illusions." "The worst enemies of real history, that is of myth, are the professional historians."

History is fiction, history is myth, myth is what man lives by. We are irresistibly reminded of Nietzsche, whom Lessing, be it said in passing, rejected as he did all rival philosophers. At all events, this is the message that he extracted from the obvious and undeniable inability of history to find the absolute about a reality which indeed it was not, according to him, worth our while searching for, since it lacked sense. The true historian's task, he thought, was to impart sense to it out of his ideals: "Ideals are the rules of our judgment, the standards by which we estimate the values of our existence, and to this extent it is ideals that think history."

No reader will expect me to agree with these views or respond to these exhortations. But they act upon me as a challenge to clarify in my own mind my attitude toward the myth.

Lessing does not believe that Clio has anything else to offer. I believe, on the contrary, that she will permit us to get nearer to the truth. This lays upon me the obligation to try to get as near to the truth as will be possible, even though I know I shall never completely attain it. As for "sense," I know that I shall have to cooperate in extracting it from the past, which in its manifold mysteriousness will often seem "senseless"; and I know that in the process something of my own will get mixed with what I find. But what I must never do is deliberately and arbitrarily impart sense to history. The sense which may in the end acquire for me a living quality must be demonstrably related, not to my own feelings, desires, or "ideals" (although to some extent it will be), but to the objective, irretrievable, and external past. That ultimately we remain faced with stark impenetrabilities does not, I repeat, darken my days; rather do the moments lighten them when I feel I have been able to lift a tip of the veil. Nor has the spectacle of generations of French historians struggling with the particular riddle of Napoleon and contradicting each other in detail as well as in general appreciation had on me a discouraging effect. I have found that spectacle characteristic of our Western civilization; that is how Western civilization proceeds.

In the book which resulted from my wartime study of French historiography on Napoleon I summed up my experience in the statement that history is "an argument without end." An argument which will not lead to any universally accepted conclusion. Starting with differing views of life and of eternity, Frenchmen are bound to differ about the great Corsican until the end of time. But that is not to say that the argument has been and will be fruitless. It has illuminated much that was dark, it has led to agreement on large tracts of the ground, and even where it has not, the points raised by each side, the suggestions and explanations about motives and character, about the immense complications in which that miraculous career was enacted, have enriched the picture. Even when the student cannot accept a particular reading, it may help to divert his mind from one-sided admiration or detraction; his mind will become aware of finer shadings where originally there was only the crude contrast between black and white. The argument, in other words, has led to a gradual even though partial conquest of reality. For that is what reading all these varied and conflicting accounts impresses on the mind—and here you have the decisive answer to Lessing, and to Sartre and Valéry as well: it is not the myths which are winning. What we are recovering by the methods of historical investigation and discussion is a real person, a real force in the realities of the past, which are, like those of the present, ever complicated and fluid, never completely to be fixed.

In October, 1945, almost exactly five years after I had been arrested by the German occupying authority, I gave a little address to my students by way of opening my lectures after that long interruption. I began by begging the young men and women to realize that criticism, fearless criticism, criticism without regard to people or nation, was the first duty of independent scholarship. That, I told them, although it might sometimes bring us into apparent conflict with other duties and other loyalties, will in reality be keeping faith with the highest values of our civilization. It is a good thing for society that there should be a group of men trained in that discipline by which the dangerous mists of fine phrases hallowed by convention can be dispelled.

I lay such stress on this [I went on] because the deceitful and insidious propaganda carried on by National Socialism against the true scholarly spirit, against criticism and the intellect, undoubtedly has left traces behind. Even now many people detect a suspicious sound in the word *intellectuals*. *Rationalism* evokes the idea of "cold"; *criticism* of "destructive." Let us try to look as if from a little distance at what the world has just passed through. We shall see that the most cold-blooded despotism and terrorism that have ever ruled and the most terrible destruction that has ever threatened European civilization have been made possible by the systematic extolling of instinct and passion above reason, by hatred and contempt for criticism. Reason and criticism are among the bulwarks of Western civilization.

A sense for criticism is a necessity, but this

is not all. A sense for tradition, love for what has grown, love and respect for what is our own—these also are needed. Is there an irreconcilable difference between this and the other? I think not, although undeniably there is a tension. At any rate this sense too, the capacity for feeling in this way, seems to me an indispensable trait in the historical attitude of mind and a precious trait in that Western civilization to which we belong.

Reason and criticism are useful and precious, but the great creative forces of life, society, and civilization lie elsewhere. Rationalists like those of the eighteenth and nineteenth centuries, who looked upon the world as a mechanism which reason could control, are an extinct species.

How are we to describe, how are we to approach those great creative forces? Here come into play deep-seated springs of conviction or faith, and our Dutch civilization, like the civilization of the entire Western world, has long passed beyond the stage of the one religion claiming the allegiance of all. But in adherents of every faith and every philosophy of life the study of history will strengthen the feeling of —how shall I put it? I said *love* and *respect* before, and I think, after all, those words will best express the mental attitude of the historian.

Without giving way to either romanticism or

fanaticism, our minds untroubled, after having allowed to criticism its full due, we shall by the spectacle of history feel strengthened our love for life, our respect for life. The true historian may detest falsehood and violence with all his soul, but facing the great movements or revolutions of history, he will neither sneer nor curse; he will before all try to understand.[9]

Now does this passage say all there is to be said from my point of view? Let me first of all admit that I am here speaking from a point of view. I know that the spectacle of the past can call forth quite different reactions. In the eighteenth century Gibbon, summarizing the depreciation current among the philosophers of his day, said, "History is, indeed, little more than the register of the crimes, follies, and misfortunes of mankind." There is in our own day Wyndham Lewis;[10] in his recent novel *Self Condemned* he pictures Professor René Harding as the man of brilliant and daring mind who, when the great "truth" suddenly dawns upon him of the hopeless idiocy of human activities solemnly recorded by historians, resigns his chair of history. "The slush and nonsense, the pillage and carnage, which we have glorified as 'history'!"

But my point of view is not, after all, a merely personal one. I began by saying, and I believe I am

9. *Historicus in de tijd*, Utrecht, 1954.
10. Wyndham Lewis, *b*. 1886 in the U. S., settled in England.

right in saying, that the attitude of mind I am attempting to define is one common to most professional historians, and I don't think the conclusion is
far-fetched when I add that it is the natural result
of the habits, the discipline, the intellectual school-
ing of our profession. History can be made to serve
every conceivable theory or temperamental pecu-
liarity. But the gloomy or despairing, the misan-
thropic or cynical reading of history is not one
which will ever stand the test of criticism or of time;
it is the essentially unhistorical reaction of individual
impatience or conceit.

Still, let me not withdraw the admission that I am
developing a theory of the use of history of which I
cannot strictly prove the universal validity. And so
I come back to my question whether the passage I
quoted from my little opening address in 1945 says
all there is to be said from my point of view. And
the answer must be not quite. The myth is a subject
that still worries me.

Looking around, the first thing I discover is that
the world's thinking is full of history mutilated or
falsified, of historical myths, which are not, on account of their remoteness from past reality, any the
less potent in the politics, national or international,
of the present. My friend Renier [11] in his *History,
Its Purpose and Method*, a book full of wit and wis-

11. G. J. Renier, *b.* 1892 in the Netherlands; professor of
Dutch History in the University of London since 1945. *History, Its Purpose and Method* appeared in 1950.

dom, assigns to history the social function of serving mankind in the capacity of that memory without which the individual would not long survive the dangers of his existence; the historian merely preserves, but the members of the community use the material preserved as and when it suits them. Yet as I see it, the historian often and rightly plays a more active part, shaping the material, suggesting, if only by implication, conclusions of importance for the present. Even so, the collective memory of the public, largely the product of the historians' teaching, is much more defective and erratic than the individual's memory of his experiences.

I wish that it were possible to draw a simple contrast between myth and history. Myth—the past arranged, without any hampering inhibition, so as to suit the prejudice of its adherents, their national or religious loyalty or intolerance, their party feeling; history—the past shown as it really was. I have said too much, and you knew too much before I said it, about the shortcomings and delinquencies of historians to pretend anything so childish. History and myth are almost inextricably mixed.

What I do say is that it has always been the ideal of historians to separate the two and that in their attempts to make their accounts conform to demonstrable, palpable truth they have done an enormous amount of useful sifting and in one field after another helped intelligible order to overcome confusion.

This order, however, will always retain an element of arbitrariness, because it is to some extent dependent on human minds. And such as it is, the history of the historians will have no more than a restricted influence on the community. Not only will the public's notions on history always lag behind those of scholarship; there sometimes seems to be downright incapacity to adopt them, largely due, no doubt, to lack of attention, though often inattention is a disguise for active reluctance. Man, after all, is not governed by reason alone, and the myth, springing from affections or hatreds, has a vitality of its own. It is a form of life.

When dealing with historical myths, traditions, or misconceptions, in the past, the historian has to accept them as manifestations of the politics or civilization of the generation to which they belong; he will extend to them the understanding, the discriminating sympathy that all manifestations of life claim from him. But the doctrine of the useful myth is, to him, of no application to the present. No doubt the historian can be so wrapped up in a myth of his own day that he does not recognize it as such; his history will suffer from it, but it does not necessarily destroy his excellence, or greatness, as a historian. By means of the one-sided or distorted interpretations determined by his prejudice he can, even for us who see through his method and reject it, throw a light upon the past by which some of its reality will be illumined. However, the historian who deliberately abandons the canons of criticism in order to build up a myth is no historian.

I have done battle with historical myths in my time. I have seen (or thought I saw) historians being led astray by blind streaks in their minds due to their devotion or their partisanship. But I have always been extremely loath to suspect any historian of wittingly falsifying or suppressing or inventing. It is the peculiar quality of the myth that it substitutes its fictional for truthful thinking, and when, for instance, G. G. Coulton, in his famous attacks on Cardinal Gasquet, used the words "falsehoods" and "lying," he did not perhaps sufficiently bear in mind the befogging effect that sentiments of loyalty and faith may have.[12] It can be maintained, of course, that to give way to this effect is a moral weakness, and certainly the plea of having honestly believed in the face of evidence to the contrary cannot with the best grace be advanced by the historian trained to detect the difference between legend and truth.

In any case, the modern critic, even though he may in the result find a value (the value that a para-

12. G. G. Coulton (1858–1947) taught ecclesiastical and medieval history as lecturer and professor at Cambridge and at Oxford; a prolific writer. The dispute with Cardinal Gasquet, 1846–1929, head of the English Congregation of Benedictines, author of many books on English ecclesiastical history, is described in Coulton's autobiography, *Fourscore Years*, 1944.

78

dox or an exaggeration sometimes has in an argument), will never admit the subjective or aprioristic method as legitimate. Undoubtedly historians have learned a great deal in recent times about how to be on their guard against the perils of subjectivism or apriorism. It is not only a matter of refined and perfected critical methods, although that certainly is of great importance. There is also the attitude of mind which appeared with Romanticism in Germany and which I have translated historism.

I have mentioned the anomalous effects caused by this new approach when allied to, or rather made captive and exploited by, philosophies and systems of various kinds. For a considerable time now most historians have been aware of the pitfalls presented by philosophies and systems. It is not that they are (as Toynbee suggested that I was) adherents of the nonsense view of history. They know quite well that it is their job (and they are driven by an irresistible human urge) to seek sense, to bring out sense, to explain, to interpret, to draw parallels and note the recurrence or appearance in similar circumstances of the phenomena that they observe. Only, they are loath to reduce it all to rigid categories, to arrange it in an imposing order. But it would be wrong to attribute this attitude of mind exclusively to the modern historian. There have always been historians like that, and one might even trace the rudiments or the remnants in the most system-ridden individuals of the tribe—it is indeed a quality inherent in the profession of history.

But the modern historian particularly is too much aware of the supremacy of life and its infinite and ever surprising variety not to be on his guard against these intellectually satisfying schemes, which may hedge in or distort the view. He will be endeavoring, above all, to preserve an open mind. He will not too readily identify a period with an idea: behind the idea he will look for the unruly, struggling men. Behind the anonymity of a class, of a nation, of a sect he will search for various shadings, for individual peculiarities. The Zeitgeist may seem to be victoriously sweeping along to the outcome known to the historian, but instead of bringing out only what seems to have contributed to that event, he will give attention also to the opponents, to the vanquished. The defeated point of view will interest him quite apart from the fact that it may not seem so utterly contemptible to future generations as its fate suggests to the worshipers of every Zeitgeist in its turn. He will remember, too, that at any moment of the past the men then living did not know what the future had in store for them, and he will let his own imagination play with alternative possibilities instead of prophesying from the event that this or that was "inevitable." He will not, in short, merely "trace lines"; he will be sensitive to the abundant fullness and to the infinite complexity.

What I venture to say is that the discipline of history, the historical spirit, is a force for truth and against myth, and that, besides, insofar as it can make itself felt, it will exercise a restraining influence, an influence making for sanity. History studied in the way I indicated will make us realize that progress has never followed a straight line; that ideals, great motive forces that they are, will in practice always lead to compromise; that there is something to be said for the other side in every dispute. I have said that historism carried to excess, as it has often been and sometimes still is, leads to a boundless relativism and a position according to which patience, tolerance, and acceptance are the only virtues. I hate every interpretation of history by which the moral issues become obscured and initiative and the personality smothered. But that is not the effect of the historical spirit as I outlined it. *Understanding* does not necessarily mean *forgiving;* the attention to the particular and the individual in despite of the idea, the Zeitgeist, or the system, leads to the very opposite of a flat picture of masses driven. Allied to it is the capacity for making distinctions. Nothing is further removed from my mind than the consideration of patience, tolerance, and acceptance as the only virtues, but fortunately it is not only in them that a bar to passionate rejection or headlong enthusiasm can be found. Who will deny that the world stands in need of such a bar? The capacity for making distinctions will provide one.

In the little speech I made to my students in October, 1945, I also said (immediately following the passage quoted above):

> Our feeling of national solidarity and patriotism does not need the stimulus of hatred. Hatred of another nation is not a historical attitude of mind. Hatred of oppression and cruelty, yes; hatred of crime and deception. But the historian who uses reason and criticism will be able to make the necessary distinction, and the rejection of an entire nation, and of that nation's civilization, which has in so many ways intertwined itself with European civilization, cannot stand the test of true historical judgment.

A state of mind, then. But this is not, of course, all that history has to offer. Men can still be seen turning to it for the other purposes I have mentioned. To almost every one of them something will respond within the mind or heart of almost every one of us. Along some of these ways, it is true, the questioner of the riddle of the past will be led more readily to myth than to history. At any rate we are still sensitive to the symbolism of historical parallels; the large view justifying the ways of God to men still exercises a fascination; the spectacle of the past can still charm our aesthetic sense; but we also find in it lessons for the practice of today, or it can be idealized in order to put the present to shame; precedents have not lost their force, and antiquity still seems vener-able, so that a demonstration of it gives a feeling of security.

But if I ask myself which are the purposes that I and I suppose most modern scholars will place first when put on our mettle to justify our calling and our work, there present themselves in answer, first, the enrichment of civilization by the reanimation of old modes of existence and thought, of which I spoke in my first and especially in my second chapter; second, the cultivation of the historical attitude of mind, of which I have just spoken; third, the elucidation of the present and its problems by showing them in perspective; and about this last point I have something more to say.

In fact, the point is closely allied to the two others, at times almost indistinguishable from them. The present is not elucidated merely by connecting it with trends in the immediately preceding period, from which it may be seen to issue. The whole of history will help us understand the world we live in. A mind that has established contact with forms of life remote and unfamiliar, that has come to know great events and personalities of some particular period, pondering motives and evidence, watching the ever surprising shapes in which greatness and character appear, or studying the curious changes of social habits and the impact of economic factors—such a mind is likely to see more deeply into contemporary phenomena and movements, be it of culture or of politics. This is what Burckhardt meant when he said that history will make us wise; for although Bacon had said the same thing three centuries before, the great Swiss historian gave to the word a somewhat different connotation by adding, "Wise for always; not clever for another time." [13] He meant, of course, that history is not to be searched for practical lessons, the applicability of which will always be doubtful in view of the inexhaustible novelty of circumstances and combination of causes, but just this, that the mind will acquire a sensitiveness, an imaginative range.

Yet undoubtedly the history of the recent past of one's own country or the group of countries belonging to the same sphere of civilization and power politics offers, for the purpose of understanding the present, a special and irreplaceable interest. There is here by universal consent [14] an immediate and practi-

13. Jacob Burckhardt, 1818–97; professor at the University of Basel, 1858–93. The dictum quoted occurs in *Weltgeschichtliche Betrachtungen* (published posthumously).

14. If Huizinga denied this (*Verzamelde Werken*, 7, 163), it was, I think, the reaction to the vogue of histories and collections of documents and memoirs relating to the first World War of a mind of exceptionally broad culture and little inclination toward politics. Now that I mention him only to indicate dissent, I feel I must add how enlightening as well as delightful I have always found his book *The Discipline of History: De Wetenschap der Geschiedenis*, 1937, now in *Verzamelde Werken*, Vol. 7.

cal use of history for anyone trying to find his way through the politics of his own or of a foreign country, or, of course, through international politics. The same might certainly be said of virtually every field of cultural or social or economic activity, but let me here limit the discussion to political history.

Politics do not start from today. They are rooted in the past. History plays its part in them, as it did in the world of the seventeenth century. Contending views of great political issues of a century and longer ago are still live issues. But also the governments, the parties, the churches, even when not a word about history is spoken, consciously or unconsciously move along tracks or find bounds set to their action which are a legacy of the past.

Better consciously than unconsciously, and that is as much as to say: better to know something about history. You may think I am merely stating a truism. Do not secretaries of state and foreign secretaries thumb the volumes of war documents published by various governments? Do they not read the biographies or memoirs of their predecessors? Will not an ambassador sent out to a country begin by reading up that country's history?

Not that a course of reading before departure to the foreign capital would be the ideal way to fit oneself for an ambassadorial post. We historians cannot give to anyone the knowledge required in capsules nicely dosed, effect guaranteed. The case of the literature about Napoleon is a propos. Always it is in the conflict of opinions, it is by comparing different views, by seeing the various aspects revolve as different minds reflect them, that history can be made to yield some of her more precious secrets. I may seem dangerously near the conclusion that only trained historians are fit to rule the world. In all sincerity that is not what I mean, although I can't deny that I have sometimes wished that, for instance, American statesmen, who now exercise so direct and profound an influence on the destinies of the world, knew more about the history of, for instance, Europe. They might not, in that case, talk so lightly about European federation. But then, many European statesmen talk lightly on that subject. Indeed, I could wish that they, too, knew their history better, or that they were gifted with a little more historical imagination.

In March, 1953, I delivered a speech at Utrecht on the three hundred and seventeenth anniversary of our university. In that speech I proclaimed my doubts about the wisdom, or even practicability, of the European federation scheme (in reality Little-European, for can one speak of Europe when England is not included?). I am relieved by what has happened since: the disappearance of the EDC from the scene of practical politics, the emergence of a combination in which England is to take her part and rash supranational experiments are eliminated. But in 1953 I soon met with the reproach that I had anticipated, namely that I was using history to advocate immobility and condemn Europe to an indefinite continuance of her plight. You see here the old conflict raising its head, the reformers denouncing history as the patron of "no-change." As it happened, I had replied to the charge beforehand in that very speech:

> By no means. I too want to go in the direction of greater European unity. What I reject are schemes taking no account of the reality. Man is both free and in bonds. Free, for he must always move on; old forms are all the time decaying; man must, and he can, use his will and choose. In bonds, for he cannot use his will indiscriminately, nor choose according to the dictates of his constructive cunning or his fancy. We are incessantly freeing ourselves from our past, but at the same time it maintains a sway over us. It is not wise policy to ignore that sway, nor should the taking it into account be denounced as a sign of rigid conservatism.[15]

It is perhaps wrong of me to broach, toward the end of a disquisition on general aspects of history, a concrete example which requires more space than I have left to do justice to its complexity. I have stated my view about that problem categorically here, and

15. Also reprinted in *Historicus in de tijd*.

indeed I hold it strongly. But the only point I am entitled to make when writing of Use and Abuse of History is that the problem shows the relevance for the present of a discussion of the past. It may be I was wrong on this question, although I think I was right. But by stating my view I took part in the discussion, the argument from which the future will emerge—the free, untrammeled argument which is what distinguishes Western civilization from that of the totalitarian states; one might almost say, which *is* Western civilization.

And I think I may add that not I personally but all professional historians do possess a kind of familiarity with the past which should not be unheard in that great argument. We do not claim to have Clio's only authentic message, but we know that we devote ourselves to the deciphering of it with a single-minded devotion. Enthusiasm and abstract thinking, too, are stating their case, supported, most likely, by mythical readings of the past. Even if we wanted to, we could not suppress those voices or prevent others from listening to them; we shall ourselves at times find in them delight and inspiration. Meanwhile, events will proceed on their mysterious course as they have always done, and to the shaping of it how much the past contributes, and how much the urge that is in man's creative powers, we can only guess. But shall historians therefore keep silent? No, we must fulfill our function, which is, to the best of our ability, to show up the myths and tell the world all we can find about past reality—in short to promote legitimate use and to check the abuse of history.

INDEX

French Revolution, 40 f., 64; as attempt to establish philosopher's heaven, 22

Gasquet, Cardinal, 78 and n.
Germany, 34, 41 f., 44
Gibbon, Edward, 74
Glorious Revolution, 21, 24
Goethe, Johann Wolfgang, 31 and n.
Grotius (Hugo de Groot), 8 and n., 9, 19; *Antiquity of the Batavian Republic*, 9, 12, 25

Hegel, G. W. F., 34 ff., 40, 43, 45 f., 49, 52, 56, 68; systematizing of historical process, 35; debt to Augustine, 35; theory of history, 35; egotism, 37; philosophic conservatism, 38
Hegelianism, 49
Herder, J. G., 25 and n., 26, 30; *Ideën zur Philosophie der Geschichte*, 25 f.
Historical method. *See* Historism
Historism (*Historismus*), 31 ff., 40, 50, 54; pitfalls, 51–2, 79
History: antinomy of, 2–3; early forms, 2–3; as producer of literature, 3; of religious books, 3–4; importance of *De civitate Dei* to, 4; purposes of study of, 4 ff.; historians of Reformation Period, 6; theological interpretation, 6–7, 44 and n., 82; political interpretation, 7 ff.; subservient to partisan controversy, 10 ff., 17, 20; educative value, 14; parochial viewpoint, 14; skepticism concerning value, 17; critical attitude applied to, 18; triumph of secular approach, 18; change in attitude toward past, 18; application of reason to study of, 18–19; course of, affected by enlightenment, 20 ff.; conflict with French Revolution, 22 ff.; Burke's view, permeating state and society, 24 f.; Herder's view of, 25 f.; concept of organic unity, 29 ff.; advocates of new vision, 30 f.; application of historical method, 32; of sympathy, 32; fallacy of the system builders, 36; Hegel and the Cosmic Spirit, 36 ff.; Marx and the economic interpretation, 42–4; Comte and science,

45–6; Positivism in Buckle and Taine, 46–7; impossibility of eliminating sentiment or egoism from, 48; modern distrust of high claims of scientific approach to, 48–9; pitfalls of historism, 51–2; Western respect for rights of history, 58; strengthening position of professional historian, 59–60; role of imagination in writing of, 60 f.; role of caution, 60; fact and causation as elements, 61 ff.; subjectivity, 62–3, 68; partial truth as best hope of historian, 63, 70; the "sense" of the past, 69–70; social value of fearless criticism, 72; the historian in the community, 75 ff.; the historian's battle with myth, 76–8; his sensitivity to the complexity of the past, 80; maintaining of moral distinctions, 81. *See also* Abuses of history, Uses of history

Hitler, Adolf, 55

Holland, 63; province of, 9, 12; Dutch history, 8, 29 n., 45 n.

Israel, history of, 13

Lessing, Theodore, 68–9, 71; *History as Giving Sense to the Senseless*, 68

Lenin, N., 44

Lewis, Wyndham, *Self Condemned*, 74 and n.

Louis Philippe, 64

Macaulay, Thomas B., 39, 41, 50, 60

De Maistre, Count Xavier, 28 and n., 33

Maitland, F. W., 62 and n.

Marx, Karl, 38, 42–4; 50; Marxism, 49, 67

Michelet, Jules, 39, 40–1, 50, 60; *History of the French Revolution*, 40

Mussolini, Benito, 55

Myth, 56, 69, 71, 75, 81 f., 89; inextricably mixed with history 76; doctrine of the useful myth, 77

Napoleon, 26, 70, 86; historiography of, 63–4

National Socialism, 55, 72

function, 3; preservation of state, 7 ff.; ethical function, 10; moral function, as storehouse of elevating *exempla*, 12 ff., 18; enriching of civilization, 14, 32 f., 83; gradual, partial conquest of reality, 71; historical spirit as a force for truth, against myth, 81; cultivation of historical attitude of mind, 83; elucidation of the present and its problems, 83 ff.